# EUROPEANS AND NATIVE AMERICANS

*Jim Corrigan*

MASON CREST
PHILADELPHIA

# NATIVE AMERICAN LIFE

# EUROPEANS AND NATIVE AMERICANS

*Jim Corrigan*

SENIOR CONSULTING EDITOR DR. TROY JOHNSON
PROFESSOR OF HISTORY AND AMERICAN INDIAN STUDIES
CALIFORNIA STATE UNIVERSITY

 MASON CREST
PHILADELPHIA

Mason Crest
450 Parkway Drive, Suite D
Broomall, PA 19008
www.masoncrest.com

CPSIA Compliance Information: Batch #NAR2013. For further information, contact Mason Crest at 1-866-MCP-Book

First printing
1 3 5 7 9 8 6 4 2

Library of Congress Cataloging-in-Publication Data

Corrigan, Jim.
  Europeans and native Americans / Jim Corrigan.
     pages cm. — (Native American life)
  Includes bibliographical references and index.
  ISBN 978-1-4222-2964-4 (hc)
  ISBN 978-1-4222-8851-1 (ebook)
  1. Indians of North America—First contact with Europeans—Juvenile literature.
  2. Indians of North America—Colonization—Juvenile literature.  3. America—Discovery and exploration—European—Juvenile literature.  I. Title.
  E98.F39C67 2013
  970.01—dc23
                                        2013007478

Native American Life series ISBN: 978-1-4222-2963-7

**Frontispiece: Statue of Massasoit, the leader of the Wampanoag people, who helped colonists from Britain establish a settlement at Plymouth in the 1620s.**

# TABLE OF CONTENTS

# INTRODUCTION

For hundreds of years the dominant image of the Native American has been that of a stoic warrior, often wearing a full-length eagle feather headdress, riding a horse in pursuit of the buffalo, or perhaps surrounding some unfortunate wagon train filled with innocent west-bound American settlers. Unfortunately there has been little written or made available to the general public to dispel this erroneous generalization. This misrepresentation has resulted in an image of Native people that has been translated into books, movies, and television programs that have done little to look deeply into the Native worldview, cosmology, and daily life. Not until the 1990 movie *Dances With Wolves* were native people portrayed as having a human persona. For the first time, native people could express humor, sorrow, love, hate, peace, and warfare. For the first time native people could express them selves in words other than "ugh" or "Yes Kemo Sabe." This series has been written to provide a more accurate and encompassing journey into the world of the Native Americans.

When studying the native world of the Americas, it is extremely important to understand that there are few "universals" that apply across tribal boundaries. With over 500 Nations and 300 language groups the worlds of the Native Americans were diverse. The traditions of one group may or may not have been shared by neighboring groups. Sports, games, dance, subsistence patterns, clothing, and religion differed—greatly in some instances. And although nearly all native groups observed festivals and ceremonies necessary to insure the renewal of their worlds, these too varied greatly.

Of equal importance to the breaking down of old myopic and stereotypic images is that the authors in this series credit Native

Americans with a sense of agency. Contrary to the views held by the Europeans who came to North and South America and established the United States, Canada, Mexico, and other nations, some Native American tribes had sophisticated political and governing structures— that of the member nations of the Iroquois League, for example. Europeans at first denied that native people had religions but rather "worshiped the devil," and demanded that Native Americans abandon their religions for the Christian worldview. The readers of this series will learn that native people had well-established religions, led by both men and women, long before the European invasion began in the 16th and 17th centuries.

Gender roles also come under scrutiny in this series. European settlers in the northeastern area of the present-day United States found it appalling that Native women were "treated as drudges" and forced to do the men's work in the agricultural fields. They failed to understand, as the reader will see, that among this group the women owned the fields and scheduled the harvests. Europeans also failed to understand that Iroquois men were diplomats and controlled over one million square miles of fur trapping area. While Iroquois men sat at the governing counsel, Iroquois clan matrons caucused with tribal members and told the men how to vote.

These are small examples of the material contained in this important series. The reader is encouraged to use the extended bibliographies provided with each book to expand his or her area of specific interest.

Dr. Troy Johnson
Professor of History and American Indian Studies
California State University, Long Beach, California

This 19th-century illustration shows one of the most important events of American history—Columbus landing in the New World in 1492.

# 1 First Contact with Native Americans

There was great excitement on that October day in the year 1492. People were running through the village, cheering and shouting as they ran toward the sea. The village chief, a man named Guacanagari, rushed out of his home and demanded to know what was causing the commotion. Three ships were approaching, he was told—three large and mysterious ships. Even more amazing, a rumor was spreading that these ships had come from the sky! Guacanagari went back inside and put on his finest clothes. As chief, it would be his job to welcome the strangers and greet their captain, who might be a god.

There was also much excitement on board the three ships. The sailors had been at sea for weeks, and were thrilled by the sight of land. They had not come from the sky, as the villagers believed. They had come from Spain. And their captain was not a god; he was an Italian explorer named Christopher Columbus. Although he did not realize it at the time, Columbus had just arrived in what would come to be known as the New World.

Columbus had set sail from Spain with his three ships—the *Santa Maria*, the *Pinta*, and the *Niña*—in search of a shorter route to Asia. He incorrectly assumed that the islands he approached were the East Indies, so he called the villagers who lived there "Indians." In fact, Columbus was nowhere near Asia. He was actually in the Caribbean Sea, and the islands he had stumbled across are known today as the Bahamas, Cuba, and the Dominican Republic and Haiti. The native peoples he encountered were the Arawak and the Caribs. Even so, the name "Indian" is still widely used today to describe Native American people.

The villagers paddled out in their canoes to meet the Spanish ships. The Spaniards' strange clothes and pale skin mesmerized them. The Spaniards were equally fascinated by the Indians' appearance. The two groups were extremely curious about one another and anxious to become friends. The Indians presented the Spaniards with trinkets made of gold, and in return, the Spaniards gave the Indians glass beads and brass bells. It was a time of celebration in the village as the Spaniards came ashore.

Although Chief Guacanagari and Christopher Columbus did not speak the same language, they soon developed a mutual respect for one another. Guacanagari gave Columbus a beautiful golden crown, a gift meant as a sign of friendship and trust. Unfortunately, Columbus did not interpret it that way. He viewed the crown as a sign that Guacanagari was handing over his land and his people to the king and queen of Spain. The golden gifts also showed Columbus that the Indians' land contained great wealth, which could be taken back to Spain. He declared that the islands now belonged to Spain and that the Indians were the subjects of King Ferdinand and Queen Isabella.

The Indians did not object to Columbus's proclamation, since they could not understand what he was saying. However, it soon became clear by their actions that the Spaniards were taking over. Helpless against Spanish armor and weapons, the Indians found themselves the victims of an invasion. Feelings of curiosity and admiration quickly turned into hatred and mistrust. Violence and death were soon to follow. Sadly, this pattern would repeat itself over and over as more Europeans arrived in the New World. ⑤

**11**

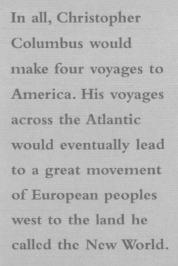

In all, Christopher Columbus would make four voyages to America. His voyages across the Atlantic would eventually lead to a great movement of European peoples west to the land he called the New World.

NATIVE AMERICAN LIFE

# 2 Cortés Conquers the Aztecs

Christopher Columbus may have been the first European explorer to set foot on Native American soil, but he certainly was not the last to do so. Less than 30 years later, a Spanish conqueror, or **conquistador**, named Hernando Cortés arrived in Mexico. Tales of riches in the New World abounded ever since Columbus had returned to Europe, and Cortés, like so many others, came seeking his fortune.

The Aztec empire was flourishing when Cortés and his army appeared in 1519. The Aztecs were a resourceful people who controlled much of Mexico. Their leader was named Montezuma, and he ruled his kingdom from a city called Tenochtitlán. Located on an island in the middle of a lake, Tenochtitlán was a remarkable city. It had many temples, schools, and houses. The Aztecs planted gardens filled with beautiful flowers and rare birds. Several bridges stretched across the lake and connected Tenochtitlán to the mainland.

The Aztec emperor Montezuma bows in respect to the seated Spanish conquistador Hernan Cortés. In 1519, Cortés landed in Mexico with a small army and proceeded to conquer the enormous Aztec empire.

Inside his palace, Montezuma worried about the newcomers. Although the white men had not yet arrived in Tenochtitlán, Montezuma was receiving disturbing reports from the east.

13

## NEW ANIMALS FOR THE NEW WORLD

Horses were not the only species that Europeans imported to America. They also brought pigs, sheep, goats, and cattle. Native Americans had never seen any of these animals before, but they soon became an important part of Indian life. Dogs had already existed in the New World, but not cats. Other creatures, such as cockroaches and rats, were unwanted stowaways from the Old World. Europeans also encountered animals they had never seen before. Alligator, raccoon, beaver, and buffalo are all examples of species indigenous to America.

The introduction of new animals, as well as new plants, changed the American landscape forever. Some native species adjusted to the change. Others could not adapt to the competition from new species and eventually became extinct. Certain animals, such as the sea otter, played important roles in European and Native American relations.

He was told the Spaniards had mysterious weapons and they rode large, strange animals called horses. (Horses did not exist in the New World until Europeans brought them.) Montezuma realized these strangers were a serious threat to his empire.

From the time he landed on the shores of Mexico, Cortés had been hearing about a beautiful city to the west that was rich with gold. Inspired by these tales, he quickly marched inland with his army. When they came within view of Tenochtitlán, the Spaniards were stunned by its splendor. As they continued to approach, Montezuma came out to greet them. Aztec prophecy foretold the return of the god Quetzalcoatl to Central Mexico. Because Cortés and his men resembled the appearance of the returned gods in the Aztec legend, Montezuma showered the men with gifts.

Cortés was impressed with Tenochtitlán and wrote a letter to the king and queen of Spain: "Your Highnesses…We have discovered a land rich in gold, pearls, and other things… There are in the city many large and beautiful houses…and many rich citizens…. And also very pleasant gardens…. Along one of the causeways to this great city run two **aqueducts** made of mortar…. Canoes paddle through all the streets…. The people of this city are dressed with… elegance and courtly bearing…. Considering that these people are barbarous, lacking knowledge of God and communication with other civilized nations, it is remarkable to see all that they have."

The Aztec ritual of human sacrifice to please their gods shocked Cortés. He considered the Aztecs to be savages, and felt no obligation to treat them with respect.

The Aztecs construct their great city, Tenochtitlán, in this 17th century painting. When Cortés arrived in Mexico in 1519, Tenochtitlán was as large as the greatest cities of Europe.

The Spanish were horrified at many of
the religious practices of the Aztecs,
especially human sacrifice. In this
drawing an Aztec priest is offering
the heart of a sacrifice to the sun god,
which the Aztecs believed needed to be
fed with blood in order to rise each day.

Despite Montezuma's hospitality, Cortés took him prisoner. Cortés then demanded all of the Aztecs' gold, and his men set out to **plunder** the city. For six months, they controlled Tenochtitlán and abused its citizens. Finally, the Aztec warriors rose up and forced the Spaniards to retreat to Montezuma's palace, where the Aztec ruler was still being held hostage. The warriors attempted to storm the palace, but failed, and Montezuma was killed during the fighting.

Realizing that they were heavily outnumbered, Cortés and his men decided to escape at night while the Aztecs slept. The Spaniards quietly crept through the darkness, out of the city. Just as they approached a bridge leading off the island, an Aztec woman who was drawing water spotted them. She yelled and screamed, waking up the warriors. As they ran, the Spaniards found themselves being struck by spears and arrows. Many fell into the water and, weighed down by stolen gold, quickly drowned. Cortés escaped, but two-thirds of his soldiers did not. The Aztecs had liberated Tenochtitlán. It was, however, only a temporary victory.

Hernando Cortés was not a man to be beaten easily. Determined to conquer the Aztecs, he rebuilt his army and found Indian allies. With over 50,000 men under his command, Cortés returned to the outskirts of Tenochtitlán. The Aztecs were ready for the assault and defended their city ferociously. Unfortunately, they were fighting more than just Cortés and his vast army. The Spaniards' previous visit to Tenochtitlán had brought an Old World disease—**smallpox**. This weakened the Aztecs considerably, but they continued to fight.

17

NATIVE AMERICAN LIFE

Their island surrounded, the Aztecs eventually began to run out of food and water. As Cortés' men attacked from the outside, disease and starvation attacked the Aztecs from inside. Still, the warriors fought on, using their arrows and spears against the Spaniards' guns and cannons.

Finally, after four months of combat, the Aztecs could fight no longer. On August 13, 1521, the siege of Tenochtitlán ended. It proved to be one of the longest continuous battles in history. The victorious Cortés ordered that the city be destroyed. Its temples and other buildings were leveled; its beautiful gardens were burned; and stone sculptures of Aztec gods were buried. Today, Mexico City stands on top of the ruins of Tenochtitlán. In fact, the president of Mexico lives in a palace located on the very spot where Montezuma's palace once stood. §

One of the reasons the Spanish could defeat the much larger Aztec army was the conquistadors' use of horses. The Aztecs had never seen these great beasts, and at first they were not sure whether horse and rider were two creatures or one. Mounted on horseback, the heavily armed and armored Spaniards were formidable in battle.

The Spanish conquistador Francisco Pizarro seizes the Inca emperor Atahualpa during a battle in the royal palace in Cajamarca, Peru. Like Cortés, Pizarro took a small army into Peru to subdue the powerful Inca empire. The conquests in Central and South America helped make Spain the wealthiest nation in Europe during the 16th and 17th centuries.

# 3 The Fall of the Inca Empire

From the beginning, Montezuma had recognized the power of the conquistadors and understood the threat these invaders brought to his kingdom. Even with knowledge of the danger, however, Montezuma was helpless to stop it. Another ruler, named Atahualpa, failed to comprehend the threat at all. Such ignorance would cost Atahualpa and his people dearly.

The Inca empire was huge, stretching for 3,000 miles along the western coast of South America. The Incas fished in the Pacific Ocean, farmed in the shadows of the Andes Mountains, and built villages in the Amazon rainforest. They were a **diverse** and organized people. The Incas traveled on paved roads, used government programs to help the poor, and developed an early type of mail service. Just as the Aztecs used pictures for record keeping, the Incas used colorful, knotted strings called *quipus.*

The Incas were already in a state of upheaval when the Spaniards arrived. The smallpox epidemic that had weakened the Aztecs had traveled south. In 1527, it reached the Incas and killed over 10 million of them, including their ruler. **Civil war** arose from the chaos, as the ruler's two surviving sons fought for control of the empire. The son who eventually won was Atahualpa.

As Atahualpa was destroying what remained of his brother's army, he received reports of the arrival of 200 white men. Such a small group seemed insignificant to Atahualpa, even if they rode horses and had strange weapons. Nevertheless, he sent an aide to observe the white men. The aide watched the Spaniards for two or three days, then returned and informed Atahualpa that they were lazy and unruly, like barbarians. Unlike many Indian cultures, the Incas were unimpressed when white men first appeared.

Francisco Pizarro, a courageous but ruthless conquistador, led the Spaniards. In 1532, they marched to a city in the mountains called Cajamarca, where Atahualpa was resting with his army. The Inca leader was not pleased with the white men's presence, but he allowed them to stay the night and agreed to meet with them the next day. However, Pizarro and his men did not sleep that night. Instead, they set up an **ambush** in the city square.

As dawn broke the next morning, the Spaniards waited for the arrival of Atahualpa. The Incas noticed that none of the white men had come outside the city square; they mistakenly assumed it was because the whites were afraid of them. Late in the afternoon, Atahualpa and over 10,000 Inca officials, lords, and servants boldly marched into the square. They were so confident, that they had not brought any weapons with them.

The meeting did not last long. A **friar** read the Requirement to Atahualpa, and shortly afterward the Spaniards opened fire. Atahualpa's nephew later described what happened:

"The Spaniards charged out with great fury into the middle of the square, where there was a high throne of the Inca, resembling a fort,

## WHY DID EUROPEAN DISEASES DO SO MUCH HARM?

Native Americans were completely isolated from the multitude of germs that roamed through Europe. The vast Atlantic Ocean protected Indians from ailments like smallpox, measles, bubonic plague, and influenza. This total isolation prevented the Indians from building any resistance. In other words, the Indians' immune systems had no idea what was coming when Europeans arrived. Diseases that had run their course in Europe would find new life in America, becoming raging epidemics that eventually killed millions.

Indians undoubtedly suffered the brunt of this biological exchange, but Europeans also encountered New World germs that would prove deadly to them. Conquistadors frequently died of malaria, and settlers suffered outbreaks of yellow fever as well as other illnesses. Regardless, the number of Europeans in America continued to grow rapidly, while at the same time Native American populations withered. In 1492, there were between 5 million and 10 million Indians living in the present-day United States. By 1890, there were only 250,000.

23

which we call an *usnu*. They occupied this and would not let my uncle ascend it. Before he reached the foot, they pulled him from his litter by force, and turned it upside down; they seized his insignia and headband, which among us is the crown, and they took him prisoner....

"That square was enclosed by walls, and all the Indians were inside like llamas. There were a great many of them and they could not get out, nor did they have any weapons—they had not brought them because of the low opinion they held of the Spaniards; all they had

Francisco Pizarro was nearly
60 years old when he led a
small force of about 200 men
through South America to the
great cities of the Incas.

## CHRISTIANITY AND THE REQUIREMENT

Religion played a major role in the European colonization of America. Friars and other religious men traveled to the New World in large numbers. Their goal was to convert the "savages" they encountered to Christianity. Most Indian cultures already had a religion of their own, however, and were unwilling to abandon it. Often, Indians would blend certain elements of Christianity with their own religion. If the friars disapproved, as they often did, the Indians would simply worship in private.

Another contribution of the Catholic Church was a document called the Requirement, signed by Pope Alexander VI in 1493. In this document, the Pope decreed that Spain was entitled to all newly discovered land. Conquistadors often read the Requirement to Indians as official notice that their land now belonged to Spain. However, the Requirement meant little to the Indians, since it was rarely translated into their language. On those occasions when it was translated, the Indians did not take it seriously. When the Requirement was read to the Inca emperor Atahualpa, he responded, "As for the Pope of whom you speak, he must be crazy to talk of giving away countries which do not belong to him."

were slings and tumis [ceremonial knives]. . . . The Spaniards killed them all—with horses, with swords, with guns—just as one might slaughter llamas, for nobody could defend himself. From more than 10,000 men there did not escape 200.

"And when all were dead they took my uncle Atahualpa to a cell, where they kept him bound all night, with a chain around his neck."

Incas did not place any monetary value on gold—to them gold and silver were merely decorative. However, Atahualpa soon recognized

that the Spaniards placed tremendous value on these metals. Atahualpa made Pizarro an offer: a roomful of gold and two rooms of silver in exchange for his freedom. Pizarro accepted the offer, and vast sums of the precious metals were brought to Cajamarca from all over the Inca empire. Although Atahualpa had kept his side of the bargain, Pizarro did not keep his and eventually had Atahualpa executed.

The slaughter in Cajamarca was not the end of the Inca empire, but it was the beginning of the end. Drawn by tales of unlimited gold and silver, Spaniards poured into South America by the boatloads. An Inca uprising several years later was somewhat successful, driving back the invaders and resulting in 1,000 Spanish deaths, but it was a short-lived victory. Just like the Aztecs, the Incas could not overcome a deadly combination of European diseases and superior technology. ⑤

27

The ruins of Machu Picchu, an Inca city high in the Andes Mountains of Peru.

John Smith and the settlers at
Jamestown trade with the neighboring
Algonquian Indians. Founded in 1607,
Jamestown became the first permanent
English settlement in North America.

# 4 Adversity in Florida and Virginia

The territory now known as the southeastern United States was more of a challenge than the Europeans had expected. The terrain was somewhat different from what they had found in Mexico, Central America, and South America. The people they found living there were different as well. Unlike the dominant Aztec and Inca civilizations, there were many unique cultures spread throughout the southeast. A conquest would require more than just defeating one emperor like Montezuma or Atahualpa.

The Spanish conquistadors started in a place they named Florida, meaning Flowery Land. The Spaniards used the word "Florida" to describe not only the state that still bears that name, but also much of the surrounding area. A small group of French adventurers made an attempt to settle in Florida, but the Spaniards quickly destroyed their settlement. This demonstrated yet another important difference from previous explorations: The Spanish would have to compete with European rivals.

The first conquistador in Florida was Ponce de León in 1513. Legend holds that Ponce de León was looking for a so-called fountain of youth, but in reality, he was only searching for gold and riches, just like the other conquistadors. Stories of brutal Spanish conquests to the south had arrived in Florida before León, so

## THE PERILOUS JOURNEY OF CABEZA DE VACA

Alvar Núñez Cabeza de Vaca was on one of the doomed rafts that set sail from Florida. He was the expedition's treasurer and kept a detailed diary. De Vaca's raft capsized during a storm. He and several other exhausted Spaniards washed up on the Gulf coast of Texas, where local Indians found them.

In his diary, Cabeza de Vaca describes what the Indians did next: "Because of the extreme coldness of the weather, they caused four or five very large fires to be placed at intervals, and at each they warmed us; and when they saw that we had regained some heat and strength, they took us to the next so swiftly that they hardly let us touch our feet to the ground. In this manner we went as far as their habitations, where we found that they had made a house for us with many fires in it."

The Spaniards were worried that they had only been saved so that they could be sacrificed to the Indian gods, but de Vaca then writes: "In the morning, they again gave us fish and roots, showing us such hospitality that we were reassured." Gradually, the Spaniards made their way westward, acting as traders and medicine men for the Indian tribes they encountered. After a six-year odyssey, Cabeza de Vaca and three of his comrades finally arrived in Mexico.

he was not welcomed there. In fact, the native people of the Calusa Nation quickly drove him away. Ponce de León returned to Florida in 1521 with 200 soldiers, but again was defeated. This time, de León had been wounded, and he died a short time later in Cuba.

Pánfilo de Narváez made the next attempt in 1528. His expedition fared only slightly better against the natives. After

31

Juan Ponce de León, who came to America with Christopher Columbus's second voyage, had helped to put down revolts by natives on the island of Hispaniola. After he discovered the island of Puerto Rico, he was in charge of overpowering the natives there. However, during his two visits to the mainland of North America, Ponce found the Native Americans more warlike. He was killed by a poisoned arrow on his second trip to Florida in 1521.

Alvar Núñez Cabeza de Vaca gazes over the desert of the American southwest. A member of a doomed Spanish expedition to Florida, Cabeza de Vaca wandered through the southwest for seven years before reaching friendly Spanish settlements in Mexico.

several months of exploring the hostile territory, Narváez and his men concluded that there was little wealth in this part of the New World. They had exhausted their supplies and were in constant danger. Desperate, they decided to build rafts and sail to the safety of Mexico. A storm scattered the rafts, and most were never heard from again. Only four survivors ever arrived in Mexico, six years after they had left Florida.

The previous failures to conquer Florida did not discourage a daring man named Hernando de Soto. A former aide to Pizarro during the Inca conquest, de Soto was not intimidated by hostile natives. In May 1539, he boldly sailed into what is now Tampa Bay with an army of 600 men, determined to crush the local Indian tribes. As they marched through Florida, de Soto and his men murdered, stole food, kidnapped chiefs, and raped Indian women. Word quickly spread among the Indian tribes that the Spaniards could be tricked into leaving by telling them that much gold and pearls could be found in a nearby village. This magical village never actually existed, but the Spaniards fell for the trick again and again.

33

## FARMING IN THE NEW WORLD

Europeans were fascinated by the strange and different foods that grew in America. Potatoes, tomatoes, and pumpkins were just a few of the plants that they had never seen before. Native Americans farmed each of these, but no single crop was as important to their culture as corn, or maize, as the Indians called it. Corn was easy to grow, and it produced a high yield. European settlers recognized the value of corn, too, and began farming it shortly after they arrived.

The settlers disapproved of Indian farming methods. Indians did not remove tree stumps from their fields, and often grew several crops mixed together in the same field. Farmers in Europe always kept neat, orderly farms with just one crop per field. By comparison, the Indian way looked messy and disorganized.

However, the settlers did not recognize the benefits of this apparent clutter. Tree stumps helped prevent soil erosion. Different crops growing together enriched the soil. Indian farmers often planted corn, beans, and pumpkins together, each one providing nutrients for the other. Cornstalks provided excellent support for the climbing bean vines, and leaves from both the corn and the beans gave shade to the pumpkins.

De Soto wandered throughout the southeast for three years, searching for wealth that he would never find. During that time, the Spaniards lost over half their men to combat or disease. Finally, in May 1542, de Soto himself became sick and died. His body was laid to rest in the Mississippi River, a river that he is credited with discovering. Just as before, the survivors returned to Mexico with nothing to show for their odyssey but tales of death and destruction.

While the conquistadors had failed in Florida, the Old World diseases that they brought with them were much more successful. As with the Aztecs and Incas, Indians living in Florida had no resistance to smallpox and other **viruses. Plagues** rapidly spread from village to village, turning them into ghost towns. Most historians agree that European germs did far more damage to Native American cultures than the Europeans themselves ever could.

Farther north, England was also beginning to explore the New World. Just as Spaniards used the word "Florida" to describe a large portion of the southeastern United States, the English used the word "Virginia" to describe an area extending from North Carolina to Canada. Unlike the conquistadors, the English arrivals were more interested in finding a place to live in the New World than in plundering it.

The first English colony was established on an island off the coast of North Carolina in 1585. The Indians who lived nearby called themselves the Roanoke, and so the island came to be known as Roanoke Island. The English settlers realized they would need the Indians' assistance in order to survive, especially since the colony's supply ship had sunk in treacherous waters near the island. The Roanoke Indians were friendly and gladly shared their hunting and farming knowledge with the settlers. In return, the settlers gave

NATIVE AMERICAN LIFE

them gifts of clothing and metal tools. The neighboring communities got along well together, at least for the first few months.

Unfortunately, Roanoke Island was not an ideal farming environment. The soil was poor, and the colonists were soon out of food. At first, the Indians were willing to share their corn supplies with the English, but by the spring of 1586, there was no longer enough corn to share. The English began to starve. Their leader, Colonel Ralph Lane, suspected that a local Indian chief was plotting against the colony. It is not known if this suspicion was correct, but in the end, Lane and a group of soldiers murdered the chief. Starving, and now fearful of retribution from the Indians, the settlers decided to abandon the colony. They left for England on the next ship.

Another attempt was made to colonize Roanoke Island a year later. Once again, the English found they could not farm the land, and became dependent on the local Indian tribes for food. Just as before, they alienated the Indians with an unprovoked attack. This time, when the ships finally arrived, there was nobody waiting to go back to England. In fact, there was no sign of the 110 settlers at all. It did not appear that they had fallen victim to an Indian attack—they just disappeared. The missing settlement became known as the Lost Colony, and white settlers avoided the area for over 100 years afterward.

Despite setbacks, England continued its efforts to establish a colony in the New World. In 1607, a site farther north was chosen

For much of his ambitious journey through Florida and the American South, Hernando de Soto and his large party of Spanish soldiers was harassed by hostile Native Americans. De Soto brought the trouble on himself by his brutal treatment of the natives he encountered.

Early attempts by the English to establish a colony on Roanoke Island failed. The people of the second colony disappeared from the island sometime between 1587 and 1590. No one is certain exactly what happened to the members of the "lost colony," but some may have joined local Indian tribes.

and it was called Jamestown. While the Jamestown land may have been more suitable for farming, its first settlers were primarily English gentlemen who did not possess basic farming skills. They, too, had to rely on the local Indians for survival. The Jamestown colony was located in territory controlled by Powhatan, a powerful chief of the Pamunkey Nation, and also the father of Pocahontas.

Powhatan and his brother Oppecancanough attempted to overthrow the colonists in 1622 and again in 1644. While they were nearly successful in 1622, the number of settlers in the Jamestown colony had increased by 1644. Furthermore, the number of warriors in Powhatan's group had decreased to a point that they stood no chance of stopping the continued takeover of Indian lands. ᔕ

# 5 From Plymouth Rock to the Great Lakes

On December 21, 1620, a group of 102 English settlers disembarked from their ship, the *Mayflower*. The settlers came to be known as Pilgrims, and they were seeking a new life in the New World. The *Mayflower* landed in Plymouth Bay of what is now present-day Massachusetts. The Pilgrims established a colony nearby called Plymouth. Legend has it that the Pilgrims first set foot in the New World on a large, granite boulder that is now known as Plymouth Rock. While there is no proof of this, the gigantic rock stands high enough on the Plymouth Bay shoreline that, at the very least, the Pilgrims must have surely noticed it.

When the Pilgrims arrived, they found no Indians, but there was much evidence that Indians had once lived there. The winter of 1620 was harsh and difficult for the Plymouth colony, as one half of the residents died from either disease or starvation. Then, in the spring of 1621, Indians appeared and greeted the colonists. The Pilgrims were shocked to find that some of the Indians spoke English. The Indians explained they had learned it from English fishermen who occasionally visited the area.

This drawing from a 17th century French book shows an Iroquois scalping a white man. The Iroquois were a powerful confederation of natives in the northeastern region of North America.

The Indians told the settlers of a great plague that had swept through the region several years earlier, killing virtually everyone. (Most likely, the plague was an Old World disease unwittingly spread by the English fishermen.) An Indian named Squanto described how the outbreak destroyed his tribe. In 1614, Squanto had been kidnapped and taken aboard an English ship to Spain, where he was sold as a slave. He eventually escaped and made his way back to his homeland, only to discover that all of his friends and family were dead.

Squanto befriended the Pilgrims and helped them endure those difficult early months. He taught them how to grow corn and showed them the best places to fish. Squanto also demonstrated how fish could be used to fertilize the soil and produce more corn. Without Squanto's assistance, the Plymouth colony might not have survived. Within a year, however, it was flourishing.

The Pilgrims learned of an Indian celebration held each year at harvest time and decided to celebrate it, too. They invited the local Indian chief, Chief Massasoit of the Wampanoag Nation, and his people to join in the festivities. For three days, the Pilgrims and the Indians feasted, played games, held contests, and gave thanks. Today, we continue to observe that same holiday—Thanksgiving.

The initial friendship and goodwill between the two cultures lasted for about 40 years. By 1662, however, thousands of new settlers had arrived and were **encroaching** on the Indians' hunting grounds. These newcomers did not have the same appreciation and

## THE ART OF WAR

Native American cultures had been fighting with one another long before the arrival of white people. Territorial disputes over hunting grounds or similar quarrels were often the cause of such conflict. However, to Indians, war was simply a means of settling an argument with a rival tribe; it was never intended to obliterate them. Many Indian cultures considered combat a sacred ritual, and it was carried out with honor and respect.

An Indian battle usually resulted in fewer casualties than a traditional European battle. Regardless, there were two Indian customs that shocked the Europeans. The practice of scalping, or cutting the skin and hair off a victim's head, and the torture of enemies captured in battle, led white observers to think of Indians as savages. Interestingly, there are many recorded instances of whites performing these very same acts.

Europeans discovered that Indian battle tactics were much better suited to the forests of America than the tactics practiced in the open fields of Europe. The Indians were masters of using trees and bushes for cover, lying in ambush, and then fleeing after a quick strike on the enemy. Europeans looked on this strategy as dishonorable, but American Revolutionaries later used it extensively against British troops in the War for Independence.

The Pilgrims and the Wampanoag celebrate the
first Thanksgiving at the Plymouth colony in
present-day Massachusetts. If not for the help of
friendly members of the Wampanoag tribe such
as Squanto, the English settlement in New
England probably would have failed.

respect for Indian ways that the Pilgrims had shown. The settlers forced their religion and government on the Indians, who became resentful. The *sachem* (chief) at that time, whom the English called King Philip, had seen enough. He quietly contacted other *sachems* and planned an uprising against the settlers.

King Philip's War began in June 1675. Tribes throughout New England assaulted and burned dozens of settlements. Terrified colonists scrambled for safety as the Indian attacks continued. At first, English attempts to stop the attacks were unsuccessful, but as time wore on and the Indians' food supplies dwindled, the tide of war shifted. Within a year, English militiamen were hunting down the Indians. Those captured were sold into slavery, including King Philip's wife and their nine-year-old son, who were sold into slavery in the West Indies. Shortly afterward, King Philip was shot and killed. His revolt against the English had failed.

A colonial leader rallies the men of Hadley, Massachusetts, during an attack by King Philip's braves in 1675.

## WHAT IS WAMPUM?

Native American cultures did not have coins or paper money the way we do today. They used small, shiny seashells that could be strung together. These shells were called wampum, and they were a critical part of Indian society.

Wampum was more than just money to the Indians. It was used for jewelry, gifts, and for communication. When council chiefs met to discuss an important issue, a belt made of wampum was used to record their decisions. A red wampum belt meant the chiefs had decided to go to war, while a white belt meant they had voted for peace. Wampum belts were kept in a public building, and Indians could learn their tribe's history just by studying the belts.

While Europeans did not understand the significance of wampum, they did know that Indians would gladly trade for it. Europeans thought the Indians were foolish for trading beaver pelts and other valuables for mere seashells. Indians thought the Europeans were foolish for exchanging large amounts of precious wampum for such common items. Eventually, Europeans learned to manufacture high-quality wampum, using glass beads instead of seashells. They even went so far as to open a wampum factory in what is now present-day New York.

King Philip had attempted to preserve his people's way of life through war. Other Native American cultures tried to preserve their way of life through peace and diplomacy. The Iroquois Confederacy, perhaps above all, understood the effectiveness of peaceful negotiation. The Iroquois Confederacy was an **alliance** of five tribes: Mohawk, Oneida, Onondaga, Cayuga, and Seneca. A sixth tribe, Tuscarora, was later admitted to the alliance, and the Iroquois Confederacy also became known as the Six Nations. This was a strong **matrilineal** society, and each tribe controlled its own section of the alliance's territory, which stretched from the city of Quebec in Canada all the way down through New York and into northern Pennsylvania.

The Iroquois Confederacy dominated the Great Lakes region long before the arrival of white people, and would continue to dominate the area long after. Aside from their size and their strength, the Six Nations knew how to deal with Europeans. Negotiations would be held with white leaders, and **wampum** would be exchanged as a sign of peace. During these talks, the goal of the Indian leaders was always to acquire as many trade goods as possible in exchange for the absolute minimum of tribal land.

The leaders of the Six Nations also recognized that there were divisions among the white men. English and French settlers, for example, were bitter rivals. The Iroquois did not hesitate to take advantage of these rivalries. When war would break out between two white factions, the Iroquois often remained neutral and profited by trading goods with both sides.

47

NATIVE AMERICAN LIFE

The Iroquois Confederacy flourished throughout the 17th and much of the 18th centuries, using careful diplomacy and clever trading tactics. Although they lost many citizens to conflict and European diseases, just like other Native American cultures, the Six Nations remained strong by accepting **refugees** from tribes whose homelands had been taken over by the settlers.

Ironically, the alliance was ultimately destroyed by a war between white men. The war was the American Revolution, and in this conflict, the Iroquois found it impossible to remain neutral. The Mohawk, Onondaga, Cayuga, and Seneca tribes supported England, while the Oneida and Tuscarora tribes sided with the American colonists. The Iroquois Confederacy had been split in two, never to be reunited again. ⑤

The Wampanoag chief Metacomet, called King Philip by English colonists in New England, led a bloody war against the European newcomers during the 1670s. However, the English were able to defend their settlements against the Indian attacks. Metacomet was killed by a British soldier in 1676.

A rocky, forest-covered cliff on Kodiak Island, Alaska. During the 18th century, Europeans encountered Native Americans while hunting for valuable furs along the coast of North America.

# The Lure of the Sea Otter

The conquistadors came to the New World in search of gold and other riches. The Pilgrims and those who followed them came in search of a place to live. In the extreme northwest, off the coast of Alaska and Canada, Europeans came in search of a different prize—the sea otter. The shiny, thick fur of the sea otter was so highly valued that traders called it "soft gold."

A string of rocky islands, named the Aleutians, juts out from Alaska into the sea. The native people of these islands, called Aleuts, made their living fishing and hunting animals such as the sea otter. They had little contact with Europeans until 1741, when a Russian naval ship arrived commanded by an explorer named Vitus Bering. The initial contact between the Russians and the Aleuts did not go well, and the Russian ship soon departed. Vitus Bering died on the journey home, but his crew returned to Russia with 600 prized sea otter **pelts.** The body of water in which the Aleutian Islands are located is now known as the Bering Sea.

Thousands of fur traders descended on the Aleutians to claim their bounty of sea otter pelts. The Russians soon realized that the Aleuts were far more skilled than they were at hunting the elusive sea otter. The Russians, therefore, decided to force the Aleuts into hunting for them. They would typically enter an Aleut village and take the women and children hostage. The Russians then told the men of the village that the hostages would only be released in exchange for a large **quota** of sea otter pelts. Often, so many pelts were required, that it would be months before the Aleut families were reunited.

By 1762, the Aleuts had endured enough of Russian aggression. On several islands, the native peoples rose up and killed a number of traders. The Russians responded viciously with their **muskets** and cannons, killing hundreds of Aleuts. Realizing they were outgunned, the Aleuts eventually ended their resistance. Instead, they focused on tolerating the invaders while still keeping as much of their original lifestyle as possible.

A similar group of people known as the Koniags refused to accept defeat. The Koniags were distant relatives of the Aleuts. They lived on Kodiak Island, located near the southern coast of mainland Alaska. Koniags prided themselves on their hardiness, learning to endure hardships from the time they were children. When the Russians arrived in 1763, the Koniags viewed them as merely another challenge.

This three-hole canoe model was made by Kodiak Island natives. To keep out the frigid water, the natives sewed themselves into their canoes, or kayaks.

The first ship that landed on Kodiak Island was treated with caution and suspicion. Once the Koniags determined the Russians' intentions, they attacked with bows and arrows. However, musket and cannon fire kept the Koniag archers too far away to do any damage. They tried again a few days later with wooden shields. But the shields offered too

little protection so the Koniags built huge, wooden barricades that sheltered 30 to 40 men each. They charged toward the ship with their heavy defenses, making it as far as the waterline before retreating under a hail of bullets. Although they had driven off the assault, the Russians knew more attacks would soon follow. They sailed away with a healthy respect for Koniag tenacity, and did not return to Kodiak Island for over 20 years.

Five centuries have now passed since Christopher Columbus stumbled upon the New World and the people he called Indians. His discovery would eventually change the lives of all Native Americans in a way they could not possibly have understood at the time. From the Incas farming in South America all the way up to the Koniags hunting sea otter off the coast of Alaska, everything would change. Life would change for the Europeans as well. Both cultures would encounter new foods, new animals, new weapons, and new lifestyles. In some instances, these exchanges benefited both participants. More often, however, the results were disastrous for Native Americans. Some disasters, such as the spread of European diseases, were unintended and inevitable. The exploitation of Native Americans by Europeans searching for land or riches was intentional, however, and could have been avoided. S

A sea otter floats in Alaskan waters. The pelts of these otters were highly valued by Russian and European trappers.

## HUNTING THE SEA OTTER

Centuries of practice helped the Aleuts develop a perfect system for tracking down the wily sea otter. Each man in the hunting party would crawl into his kayak and paddle out to sea. When one spotted an otter, he silently raised his paddle high above his head. The other hunters paddled over quietly so as not to alarm their prey. They formed a circle around the spot where the otter had been seen and patiently waited for it to come to the surface for air.

When the creature finally surfaced, the hunters hurled their spears at it. Aleuts were excellent marksmen who could often hit their target at distances of up to 100 feet. If they missed, they would tighten the circle and wait for the sea otter to reappear. This process continued until the exhausted otter finally succumbed. The hunter whose spear had struck first was entitled to claim the otter as his own, but he usually shared the prize with his companions.

The Aleuts wasted little of the sea otter, eating the meat and using its fur for clothing. Europeans, on the other hand, did not like the taste of sea otter meat, and were interested only in the valuable pelt.

# CHRONOLOGY

**1492**    Christopher Columbus accidentally discovers the New World while looking for a shorter route to Asia.

**1513**    Juan Ponce de León attempts to conquer Florida, but is driven away by the local Indians.

**1519**    Hernan Cortés and his army arrive in Mexico.

**1521**    August 13, Cortés conquers the Aztec capital of Tenochtitlán after a four-month battle; Ponce de León makes another attempt to conquer Florida, but fails and dies in the attempt.

**1527**    An epidemic of smallpox, brought by Europeans to the New World, kills over 10 million Incas.

**1528**    Another unsuccessful attempt to conquer Florida is made, this time by Pánfilo de Narváez.

**1532**    Francisco Pizarro and his men defeat the Inca armies; they later execute the Inca ruler, Atahualpa.

**1539**    Hernando de Soto begins a three-year rampage through Florida and surrounding areas in search of gold and pearls.

**1585**    The English colony of Roanoke is established on an island near the coast of North Carolina; it is soon abandoned.

**1587** A second attempt is made to colonize Roanoke Island; however, within three years the Roanoke settlers have disappeared from the colony.

**1607** The English colony of Jamestown is founded. With the help of an Algonquian chief named Powhatan, Jamestown prospers, becoming the first permanent English settlement in North America.

**1620** The Pilgrims arrive in Plymouth on December 21. Friendly Wampanoag natives assist the colonists in building their settlement.

**1675** King Philip's War, an Indian uprising in New England, begins, but the Indians are defeated within a year.

**1741** The first Russian ship lands on the Aleutian Islands; Russian traders would soon begin exploiting the Aleuts.

**1762** Aleuts revolt against the Russian fur traders, but fail to drive them out.

**1763** The Koniags successfully force Russian invaders from Kodiak Island near Alaska.

# GLOSSARY

**Alliance** an association to further the common interests of the members.

**Aqueduct** a conduit for water; especially one for carrying a large quantity of flowing water.

**Ambush** an unexpected attack from a concealed position.

**Civil war** a war between opposing groups within a country.

**Codices** picture books used by the Aztecs to record events.

**Conquistador** the Spanish word for conqueror.

**Diverse** composed of distinct elements or qualities.

**Encroach** to intrude gradually or stealthily, often taking away somebody's authority, rights, or property.

**Friar** a male member of a religious order.

**Matrilineal** tracing descent through the maternal (mother's) line.

**Musket** a shoulder gun with a long barrel and smooth bore, used between the 16th and 18th centuries.

**Quota** the number or amount constituting a proportional share.

**Pelt** the skin of an animal, often with the hair, skin, or wool still attached.

**Plague** a disease that spreads very rapidly, infecting and killing large numbers of people.

**Plunder** to rob a place or the people living there, or steal goods using violence and causing damage.

**Refugee** somebody who is seeking to escape war or persecution by going to a foreign country.

**Smallpox** an infectious disease from Europe that killed millions of Native Americans.

**Virus** a small particle that lives as a parasite in plants, animals, and bacteria and causes disease.

**Wampum** small, shiny seashells that North American Indians used for trade, ceremony, and record keeping.

# FURTHER READING

DuVal, Kathleen. *The Native Ground: Indians and Colonists in the Heart of the Continent*. Philadelphia: University of Pennsylvania Press, 2006.

Jennings, Matthew. *New Worlds of Violence: Cultures and Conquests in the Early American Southwest*. Knoxville: University of Tennessee Press, 2011.

Jones, David, and Brian Molyneaux. *The Illustrated Encyclopedia of American Indian Mythology: Legends, Gods and Spirits of North, Central, and South America*. Leicester, U.K.: Anness, 2010.

Levy, Buddy. *Conquistador: Hernan Cortes, King Montezuma, and the Last Stand of the Aztecs*. New York: Bantam Books, 2008.

MacQuarrie, Kim. *The Last Days of the Incas*. New York: Simon and Schuster, 2007.

Oberg, Michael Leroy. *Native America: A History*. Malden, U.K.: Blackwell Publishing, 2010.

Philbrick, Nathaniel. *Mayflower: A Story of Courage, Community, and War*. New York: Viking, 2006.

# INTERNET RESOURCES

**http://www.csulb.edu/colleges/cla/departments/americanindianstudies/faculty/trj**

Website of the American Indian Studies program at California State
University, Long Beach, which is chaired by Professor Troy Johnson. The
site presents unique artwork, photographs, video, and sound record-
ings that accurately reflect the rich history and culture of Native
Americans.

**http://www.fordham.edu/halsall/source/columbus1.html**

At this site, which is sponsored by Fordham University, you can read
from the journal of Christopher Columbus as he describes his legendary
voyage of 1492.

**http://www.pilgrimhall.org**

Learn more about the *Mayflower*, the first Thanksgiving, and everyday
Pilgrim life.

**http://nmai.si.edu/home**

This site contains fascinating information collected by the Smithsonian
Institution about Native American history and culture.

Publisher's Note: The websites listed on this page were active at the time of
publication. The publisher is not responsible for websites that have changed
their address or discontinued operation since the date of publication. The
publisher reviews and updates the websites each time the book is reprinted.

# INDEX

NATIVE AMERICAN LIFE

# PICTURE CREDITS

# CONTRIBUTORS

**Dr. Troy Johnson** is chairman of the American Indian Studies program at California State University, Long Beach, California. He is an internationally published author and is the author, co-author, or editor of twenty books, including *Wisdom Spirits: American Indian Prophets, Revitalization Movements, and Cultural Survival* (University of Nebraska Press, 2012); *The Indians of Eastern Texas and The Fredonia Revolution of 1828* (Edwin Mellen Press, 2011); and *The American Indian Red Power Movement: Alcatraz to Wounded Knee* (University of Nebraska Press, 2008). He has published numerous scholarly articles, has spoken at conferences across the United States, and is a member of the editorial board of the journals *American Indian Culture and Research and The History Teacher.* Dr. Johnson has served as president of the Society of History Education since 2001. He has won awards for his permanent exhibit at Alcatraz Island; he also was named Most Valuable Professor of the Year by California State University, Long Beach, in 1997 and again in 2006. He served as associate director and historical consultant on the award-winning PBS documentary film *Alcatraz Is Not an Island* (1999). Dr. Johnson lives in Long Beach, California.

**Jim Corrigan** is a freelance writer and historian from Harrisburg, Pennsylvania. He has authored numerous magazine articles, newspaper articles, and book reviews. He specializes in Native American history and American military history.